Under A Soprano Sky

Sonia Sanchez

Africa World Press, Inc.

P.O. Box 1892
Trenton, New Jersey 08607
(609) 695-3766

Africa World Press, Inc.
P.O. Box 1892
Trenton, N.J. 08607

Copyright ©Sonia Sanchez, 1987

First Published in 1987

Cover design and illustrations by:
Adjoa Jackson-Burrowes

Photo by: Gordon R. Robotham

Typeset by TypeHouse of Pennington

Library of Congress Catalog Card Number:
87-70962

ISBN: 0-86543-052-7 Cloth
       0-86543-053-5 Paper

Acknowledgements: Some of the poems in
this collection have already appeared in
Callaloo, Against the Current 8, March-April
1987, The Berkeley Poetry Review, Issue #20,
The Pennsylvania Review, Fall 1985.

Acknowledgement

for my brother Wilson Driver, Jr.
and for my father, Wilson L. Driver.

Contents

Beginnings

Section One

Section Two

Beginnings

under a soprano sky

1.

once i lived on pillars in a green house
boarded by lilacs that rocked voices into weeds.
i bled an owl's blood
shredding the grass until i
rocked in a choir of worms.
obscene with hands, i wooed the world
with thumbs
                    while yo-yos hummed.
was it an unborn lacquer i peeled?
the woods, tall as waves, sang in mixed
tongues that loosened the scalp
and my bones wrapped in white dust
returned to echo in my thighs.

i heard a pulse wandering somewhere
on vague embankments.
O are my hands breathing? I cannot smell the nerves.
i saw the sun
ripening green stones for fields.
O have my eyes run down? i cannot taste my birth.

2.

now as i move, mouth quivering with silks
my skin runs soft with eyes.
descending into my legs, i follow obscure birds
purchasing orthopedic wings.
the air is late this summer.

i peel the spine and flood
the earth with adolescence.
O who will pump these breasts? I cannot waltz my tongue.

under a soprano sky, a woman sings,
lovely as chandeliers.

3

Section One

So much have been said, so little being done
they still killing people and they having,
having having lots of fun. Killing the people,
having their fun. . . . .
—Bob Marley

A poem for my brother
   (reflections on his death from AIDS:
   June 8, 1981)

1. death

The day you died
a fever starched my bones.
within the slurred
sheets, i hoarded my legs
while you rowed out among the boulevards
balancing your veins on sails.
easy the eye of hunger
as i peeled the sharp
sweat and swallowed wholesale molds.

2. recovery (a)

What comes after
is consciousness of the morning
of the licensed sun that subdues
immoderate elements.
there is a kindness in illness
the indulgence of discrepancies.

reduced to the ménage of houses
and green drapes that puff their seasons
toward the face.
i wonder what to do now.
i am afraid
i remember a childhood that cried
after extinguished lights
when only the coated banners answered.

3. recovery (b)

There is a savior in these buds
look how the phallic stems distend
in welcome.
O copper flowerheads
confine my womb that i may dwell within.

9

i see these gardens, whom i love
i feel the sky's sweat on my face
now that these robes no longer bark
i praise abandonment.

4. wake

i have not come for summary.
must i renounce all babylons?
here, without psalms,
these leaves grow white
and burn the bones with dance.
here, without surfs,
young panicles bloom on the clouds and fly
while myths tick grey as thunder.

5. burial

you in the crow's rain
rusting amid ribs
my mouth spills your birth
i have named you prince of boards
stretching with the tides.

you in the toad's tongue
peeling on nerves
look. look. the earth is running palms.

6. (on) (the) (road). again.

somewhere a flower walks in mass
purchasing wholesale christs
sealing white-willow sacraments.

naked on steeples
where trappist idioms sail
an atom peels the air.

O i will gather my pulse
muffled by sibilants
and follow disposable dreams.

haiku
   (for a blk/prostitute)

redlips open wide
like a wound winding down on
the city. clotting.

elegy
  (for MOVE* and Philadelphia)

    1.

philadelphia
  a disguised southern city
squatting in the eastern pass of
colleges cathedrals and cowboys.
philadelphia. a phalanx of parsons
and auctioneers
  modern gladiators
erasing the delirium of death from their shields
while houses burn out of control.

    2.

c'mon girl hurry on down to osage st
they're roasting in the fire
smell the dreadlocks and blk/skins
roasting in the fire.

c'mon newsmen and tvmen
hurryondown to osage st and
when you have chloroformed the city
and after you have stitched up your words
hurry on downtown for sanctuary
in taverns and corporations

and the blood is not yet dry.

    3.

how does one scream in thunder?

———————————

*MOVE: a philadelphia based back to nature group whose head-
quarters was bombed by the police on May 13, 1985, killing men,
women and children. An entire city block was destroyed by fire.

12

4.

they are combing the morning for shadows
and screams tongue-tied without faces
look. over there. one eye
escaping from its skin
and our heartbeats slowdown to a drawl
and the kingfisher calls out from his downtown capital
And the pinstriped general reenlists
his tongue for combat
and the police come like twin seasons of drought and flood.
they're combing the city for lifeliberty and
the pursuit of happiness.

5.

how does one city scream in thunder?

6.

hide us O lord
deliver us from our nakedness.
exile us from our laughter
give us this day our rest from seduction
peeling us down to our veins.

and the tower was like no other.   amen.
and the streets escaped under the
cover of darkness   amen.
and the voices called out from
their wounds   amen.
and the fire circumsized the city   amen.

7.

who anointeth this city with napalm?   (i say)
who giveth this city in holy infanticide?

13

8.

beyond the mornings and afternoons
and deaths detonating the city.
beyond the tourist roadhouses
trading in lobotomies
there is a glimpse of earth
this prodigal earth.
beyond edicts and commandments
commissioned by puritans
there are people
navigating the breath of hurricanes.
beyond concerts and football
and mummers strutting their
sequined processionals.
there is this earth. this country. this city.
this people.
collecting skeletons from waiting rooms
lying in wait. for honor and peace.
one day.

Poem
South african
children braided
in a colony
of charred scarecrows

Morning raga: 6/28/84

did you see the news tonite?
james r. thornwell died today
of an epileptic fit. 41 year old
blackman. ex/vietnam/veteran.
given lsd in the service spliced
his own genes reproduced himself
in manic depressive colors and
was discharged. jasrthornwell
died today. never worked again.
became a drifter. while his mind
drilled in military sermons and
drugs stepped out of his immaculate
flesh and hummed . . . . . .

haiku
(for Osage ave
and Doorknop)

coastlines of powdered
bones run side by side turning
into black cobwebs.

Philadelphia: Spring, 1985

1.

*/a phila. fireman reflects after
seeing a decapitated body in the MOVE ruins/*

to see those eyes
orange like butterflies
over the walls.

i must move away
from this little-ease
where the pulse
shrinks into itself
and carve myself in white.

O to press the seasons
and taste the quiet juice
of their veins.

2. */memory/*

a.

Thus in the varicose town
where eyes splintered the night with glass
the children touched at random
sat in places where legions rode.

And O we watched the young birds
stretch the sky
until it streamed white ashes
and O we saw mountains lean on seas
to drink the blood of whales
then wanter dumb with their wet bowels.

b.

Everywhere young
faces breathing in crusts.

breakfast of dreams.
The city, lit by a single fire,
followed the air into disorder.
And the sabbath stones singed our eyes
with each morning's coin.

      c.

Praise of a cureless death they heard
without confessor;
Praise of cathedrals
pressing their genesis from priests;
Praise of wild gulls who came and drank
their summer's milk,
then led them toward the parish snow.

How still the spiderless city.
The earth is immemorial in death.

haiku
   (for the police on osage ave)

they came eating their
own mouths orgiastic teeth
smiling crucifixions

At the Gallery of La Casa De Las Americas
Habana. dec. 1984

Picture No. 1
Arnold Belkin: Attica

You say Belkin that the bones
keep regenerating themselves
but these zeromen surrounding us
will they always allow us time to
recruit marrow for our bones
packaged in attica mold.
Will we always stitch ourselves
together in time Belkin as these
spacemen jailers freeze their
penises in future containers
to be opened in perpetuity.
Stepping back from your picture
Belkin i remember my last visit
to attica the bullet holes loitering
in the walls the sound of bullets
still circling our eyes.

Picture No. 2
Roberto Malta: Chile: Sin Titulo

Comic strip phantoms polluting
the earth with freudian cartoons
dr seuss daddies in crisis.
bleep bleep bleep
calling all saturdaymorning
redwhiteandblueamerican kids
slig spliggety sploo
calling all yall bloods
comeincomein whereeveryouare
hee. hee. haa. And yo mama too.

They're barbecuing ribs this morning
a good sale on 4th of july ribs today
mothers fetuses at half-price
the little black bastards ain't
worth shit nohow.
sitting on top of the world the
stone people sit like pelicans
holier than time.

it's raining clasped hands again.

the acrobatic preachers have
returned wearing their baggy
pants smiles
in the name of general motors
mcdonalds the pope the father
son and holy ghost.
in the name of holidays and genocide
parades infanticide and imperialism
we bless this wholewideworld
of sports and what's left over
is up for grabs.

22

to have prayed for a second coming
and found you waiting in the wings
with sylvester trying to catch tweety-bird.
    i thot i saw a putty cat.
    i diiid see a putty cat.
c'mon everybody.
       let's dive for cover.

Section Two

We have to learn to remember
what the clouds cannot forget.
—Nicolás Guillén

"también como la tierra
yo pertenezco a todos.
no hay una sola gota
de odio en mi pecho. abiertas
van mis manos
esparciendo las uvas
  en el viento.
        —pablo neruda

(like the earth, I
belong to everyone.
there is not a
single drop of hatred
in my breast.
open wide my
hands scatter
grapes to the wind.)
                    —pablo neruda

:this is a tarot reading:
for robert buttel on the
occasion of his retirement
from temple university

1.

i see you grafting these temple towers
with formulaic fables and
yeatsian mysteries.
you trained in sacrifice resurrect
his male umbilicus threading rebellion
through fluids strong enough to float words.
london bridge still is not falling down.
in this colony of domestic scars
memories ache when it rains.

2.

what is the correct card for the poet?
was he the knight of swords the
beggarmanmagician strip-mining
tongues in gaelic magic?
am i the three of cups echoing on waves
like yemayá, through the ninth month on
the ninth day on a river of spades?
how shall we shuffle our wounds?

3.

when the emperor sets in the rain
and catches the sun,
when the lectures fall from your eyes
like unwanted saliva,
when the astonished skin shreds
in early morning fists,

you will remember to laugh in braille.

4.

come step in the flames with
us   our spines metal on
metal praise poems.

haiku
   (for morani and mungu)

we make our own
way to birth asking which is
the long walk to death.

3 X 3

shigeko: a hiroshima maiden speaks:

i have been amid organized death that hurried
i have been at sea among charitable waves
i have been forgotten by those who once knew me
i have been alone.
i have been under bleached skies that dropped silver
i have been open flesh replaced by commemorative crusts
i have been taped.
i have been specific among generalities
i have been fed residual death in a bottle
i have been in mourning for sterile faces
i have been obliged.

3 X 3

Carl: a Black man Speaks:

i come from white shadows that hide my indigence
i come from walking streets that are detoured
i come from pushing wagons that do not turn
i come from indifference.
i come from uncut cloth that patterns me
i come from vague violets gift-wrapped by slum parked thoughts
i come from hate.
i come from men who assume no responsibilities
i come from their wives who claw in the darkness
i come from white spit foaming with militant bubbles
i come from hell.

3 X 3

the poet speaks after silence:

i am going among neutral clouds unpunctured
i am going among men unpolished
i am going to museums unadorned
i am going home.
i am going to charge congenital poverty
i am going to hold young heads in my hands
   and turn them slowly
i am going to cry.
i am going amid striped weaves forever winding
i am going unstyled into a cave
i am going in the bluerain that drowns green crystals
i am going to die.

insomnia

i hear the wind of graves moving the sky.
the hills level their priested black
toward the vehement morning.
pain swears above the city.
from galleries of night
unvarnished dreams ring past these giant cuts
and as i kiss the eunuch moon,
the earth is out of my eyes.

"There is no news from Auschwitz"
    New York Times article by A.M. Rosenthal
                                    1958

along that funeral plain
green wipes away old waves
that rolled the eyes
and tangled flowers veil vile kennel dust
bequeathed to dawns.
the years are done.
the earth bent toward canals bears
sterile bowels repenting woven eyes
while bone-filled drifts that scattered blood
yield other births.
death is not there: no special people
trailing alien dens,
or children moving in the rain of ash
unravelling minds.
life is not there: not even myths that rode
young stallions to a circus tent
and carried torches on a convent wire
beyond the tides.
no other signs that men patrol chained
sheets of sea.
i grieve our empty ships.
there is no news from Auschwitz.

question
(for mrs. rinaldi)

you wonder if i knew
stephen?
  no more than the
other children racing
in the halls.
    you wonder if
we spoke.
  by chance
  today
he asked me for a
pen
  cil seconds
  on pancakes.
    and when i
tried to breath
back ten years
into his mouth
  i tasted
his morning meal.
    you wonder
if i knew stephen?

fragment 3

come all you late twenty
year olds you young thirties
and forties and fifties.
O lacquered revolutionists!
all you followers of vowelled
ghosts painted on neon signs.
O noise of red bones cascading dreams.

come to conscripted black
mounted on a cell of revelation
come and salute death
while the rust of tombs
murmur old sonnets
and my grave sinks with
the pleasure of insects
who wear no diadem.

words
   (for mr. and mrs. rinaldi)

i saw death
   today
and didn't know what
to do with it.
   obscene/
      yellowish/
         death
lounging on a pennsylvania
farm.
   i screamed at death
      today
but my words ran down
against autumn's
   fast pace.
      i know nothing
of here/
   after songs
      of space/filled with souls.
i know only
   that children bloom
      and fade like
         flowers
and that death is a six
o'clock door
   forever changing time.

poet

i met a poet
who had lived in mexico
for awhile,
and he brought picture-postcard
poems about jíbaros
who brought their guts to cool
under a madonna's shawl.
but i had seen benito alizraki
peel a mother and son toward
self-service shrines
where purple acrobats blinded
the slow eyes and turned them
ecstatic toward their
packaged excrement.

the inmate

i shall go home today. i am not laughing
my brain is done with dividing the
hilarious from the humorous. i
shall sit at this desk of sanity and
never clean the curtained windows of
a red room where decorated fingers
punctured my intangible reflexes.
i am quiet as the frail green recently
promoted from her cell of frosts. i am
calm as the spreading rain of spring paints
new stripes toward reclaimed targets.
O this white rain will flood the vacant rooms
once leased by reserved apparitions.
i shall go home today and all i require
is tall boots before i disturb the grounded
snow that alerts me.

Section Three

in the old age black was not counted fair
or if it were, it bore not beauty's name.
                              —Shakespeare

in blackness there is great virtue
if you will but observe its beauty
                                    —Antar

Last recording session/for papa joe

don't be so mean papa
cuz the music don't come easily now
don't stomp the young dude
straining over his birthright.
he don't know what he doing yet
his mornings are still comin
one at a time
don't curse the night papa joe
cuz yo beat done run down
we still hear yo fierce tides
yo midnight caravans singing tongues into morning.
don't be so mean man
one day he'll feel the thunder in yo/hands
yo/arms wide as the sea
outrunning the air defiantly.
you been ahead so long
can't many of us even now
follow the scent you done left behind.
don't be so mean man un less
you mean
   to be mean
     to be
      me
  when you mean
    to be
      mean.

two haiku
  (for Clarence H. Watson and
  The Count)

   1.

you and The Count walked
straight up drank the waters of
the underworld. Sailed

   2.

you came forth by day
praising the nite with music
giving our ears souls.

tanka
   **(for papa Joe Jones who used to
   toss me up to the sky)**

sailing upward i
crease the air see you look a/
way. yo spastic arms
in conversation with the day
turn to catch my yellow lips.

haiku
    (walking in the rain in Guyana)

watusi like trees
holding the day like green um/
brellas catching rain.

on listening to Malcolm's Ballot or The Bullet

make it plain brother
malcolm sweet singer
of tongues that loosen
the scalp. show me how
to be a revolutionary
overnight. wrap me in your
red orange rage
til i ripen in your black field.
O masculine man of words
your words run down
and no one can wind
you up again.

haiku
    (for domestic workers
    in the african diaspora)

i works hard but treated
bad   man. i'se telling you de
truth   i full of it.

Song No. 3
(for 2nd & 3rd grade sisters)

cain't nobody tell me any different
i'm ugly and you know it too
you just smiling to make me feel better
but i see how you stare when nobody's watching you.

i know i'm short black and skinny
and my nose stopped growin fo it wuz 'posed to
i know my hairs short, legs and face ashy
and my clothes have holes that run right through to you.

so i sit all day long just by myself
so i jump the sidewalk cracks knowin i cain't fall
cuz who would want to catch someone who looks like me
who ain't even cute or even just a little tall.

cain't nobody tell be any different
i'm ugly anybody with sense can see.
but. one day i hope somebody will stop me and say
looka here. a pretty little black girl lookin' just like me.

Dear Mama,

It is Christmas eve and the year is passing away with calloused feet. My father, your son and I decorate the night with words. Sit ceremoniously in human song. Watch our blue sapphire words eclipse the night. We have come to this simplicty from afar.

He stirs, pulls from his pocket a faded picture of you. Blackwoman. Sitting in frigid peace. All of your biography preserved in your face. And my eyes draw up short as he says, "her name was Elizabeth but we used to call her Lizzie." And I hold your picture in my hands. But I know your name by heart. It's Mama. I hold you in my hands and let time pass over my face: "Let my baby be. She ain't like the others. She rough. She'll stumble on gentleness later on."

Ah Mama. Gentleness ain't never been no stranger to my genes. But I did like the roughness of running and swallowing the wind, diving in rivers I could barely swim, jumping from second story windows into a saving backyard bush. I did love you for loving me so hard until I slid inside your veins and sailed your blood to an uncrucified shore.

And I remember Saturday afternoons at our house. The old sister deaconesses sitting in sacred pain. Black cadavers burning with lost aromas. And I crawled behind the couch and listened to breaths I had never breathed. Tasted their enormous martyrdom. Lives spent on so many things. Heard their laughter at Sister Smith's latest performance in church—her purse sailing toward Brother Thomas's head again. And I hugged the laughter round my knees. Draped it round my shoulder like a Spanish shawl.

And history began once again. I received it and let it circulate in my blood. I learned on those Saturday afternoons about women rooted in themselves, raising themselves in dark America, discharging their pain without ever stopping. I learned about women fighting men back when they hit them: "Don't never let no mens hit you mo than once girl." I learned about "womens waking up they mens" in the nite with pans of hot grease and the compromises reached after the smell of hot grease had penetrated their sleepy brains. I learned about loose women walking their abandoned walk down front in church, crossing their legs instead of their hands to God. And I crept into my eyes. Alone with my daydreams of being woman. Adult. Powerful. Loving. Like them. Allowing nobody to rule me if I didn't want to be.

And when they left. When those old bodies had gathered up their sovereign smells. After they had kissed and packed up beans snapped and cakes cooked and laughter bagged. After they had called out their last goodbyes, I crawled out of my place. Surveyed the room. Then walked over to the couch where some had sat for hours and bent my head and smelled their evening smells. I screamed out loud, "ooaweeee! Ain't that stinky!" and I laughed laughter from a thousand corridors. And you turned Mama, closed the door, chased me round the room until I crawled into a corner where your large body could not reach me. But your laughter pierced the little alcove where I sat laughing at the night. And your humming sprinkled my small space. Your humming about your Jesus and how one day he was gonna take you home . . .

Because you died when I was six Mama, I never laughed like that again. Because you died without warning Mama, my sister and I moved from family to stepmother to friend of the family. I never felt your warmth again.

But I knew corners and alcoves and closets where I was pushed when some mad woman went out of control. Where I sat for days while some woman raved in rhymes about unwanted children. And work. And not enough money. Or love. And I sat out my childhood with stutters and poems gathered in my head like some winter storm. And the poems erased the stutters and pain. And the words loved me and I loved them in return.

My first real poem was about you Mama and death. My first real poem recited an alphabet of spit splattering a white bus driver's face after he tried to push cousin Lucille off a bus and she left Birmingham under the cover of darkness. Forever. My first real poem was about your Charleswhite arms holding me up against death.

My life flows from you Mama. My style comes from a long line of Louises who picked me up in the nite to keep me from wetting the bed. A long line of Sarahs who fed me and my sister and fourteen other children from watery soups and beans and a lot of imagination. A long line of Lizzies who made me understand love. Sharing. Holding a child up to the stars. Holding your tribe in a grip of love. A long line of Black people holding each other up against silence.

I still hear your humming Mama. The color of your song calls me home. The color of your words saying, "Let her be. She got a right to be different. She gonna stumble on herself one of these days. Just let the child be."

And I be Mama.

A Poem for a Black Boy
  (For andrew waiting for a bus
  on a mt. airy corner)

What if they close their
windows as you walk
near their cars?
What if they lock their
doors and stare saliva stares?
On this cold december morning
waking up from stars
you are the wind choreographing our flesh
you are the sacred water baptizing our tongues.

Section Four

your mouth was the daylight and dark of my world,
your skin, the republic i shaped for myself with kisses.

—pablo neruda

fall

i have been drunk since
summer, sure you would
come to sift the waves
until they flaked like
diamonds over our flanks.
i have not moved.
even when wild
horses, with snouts like pigs
came to violate me,
i squatted in
my baptism.
O hear the sea
galloping like stallions
toward spring.

tanka

these bluegreen waves are
licking me clean like you do
when you kneel kiss my
opening lips and i feel
the murmur of your sea... entering

tanka

like dark old men the
pomp of our passion is
mere ceremony
and each day is drowned in a
procession of polished pain.

fragment 1

alone
deranged by loitering
i hear the bricks pacing my window.
my pores know how to come.
what survives in me
i still suspect.

how still this savior.
white suit in singing hand.
spitting mildew air.
who shapes the shade
is.

i am a reluctant ache
authenticating my bones.
i shall spread out my veins
and beat the dust into noise.

haiku

my body is full
it whistles a cool attack
but not with your noise.

fragment 2

i am reciting the rain
caught in my scream.
these lips cannot swim
only by breasts wild as
black waves.

i met a collector of rain   once
who went to sleep in my sleeve.
is his alibi still under
my arm?

i keep coughing up butterflies
my entrails trail albino tunes
his voice comes in my hair.
is the flesh tender where the knees weep?

haiku

like ermine when i
come to lick your winter salt
my tongue freezes in blood.

short poem: at midnite

however i secure my life
whenever i drink or eat
whatever i sense through the doors of my head
my luck is short like dust.
whenever i meet my eyes in travel
whomever i love
wherever i taste the world
my life blushes red.

haiku

man. you write me so
much you bad as the loanhouse
asking fo they money

towhomitmayconcern

watch out fo the full moon of sonia
shinin down on ya.
git yo/self fattened up man
you gon be doing battle with me
ima gonna stake you out
grind you down
leave greasy spots all over yo/soul
till you bone dry. man.
you gon know you done been touched by me
this time.
ima gonna tatoo me on you fo ever
leave my creases all inside yo creases
i done warned ya boy
watch out
for the full moon of sonia
shinin down on ya.

haiku

i want to make you
roar with laughter as i ride
you into morning.

short poem 3

was it yesterday we shifted the air
and made it blossom?
O the raucous petals loud as a prairie song.
what was the elaborate sweat,
the picnics of the poor
the eyes that clapped the silence?
where was the wisdom of breaths contained
in straw?
O is it you now
pausing in profile inspecting
my wolf dreams?

blues

will you love me baby when the sun goes down
i say will you love me baby when the sun goes down
or you just a summer time man leaving fo winter comes round.

will you keep me baby when I'm feeling down 'n' out
i say will you hold me baby when i'm feeling down 'n' out
or will you just stop & spit while i lives from hand to mouth.

done drunk so much of you i staggers in my sleep
i say done drunk so much of you man, i staggers in my sleep
when i wakes up baby, gonna start me on a brand new week.

will you love me baby when the sun goes down
i say will you love me baby when the sun goes down
or you just a summer time man leaving fo winter comes round.

summerpoem: 1986

1
memory i alone know
moving on hills
where colored tombs display their void,
and grass dipped in the parish rose
conclude design.

earth. tight as a grape, begins to peel
spitting long metal seeds
spilling black juice among her ruins.
the girl, christened by suns,
wheels from the shore to wade her rivers

2
and then to wander
like quicksand over the fields
and then to bear the island stars
and tuck them blessed among stables.
golden rang her pulse.

3
in her season
she painted violets
and drank their deep channels.

Sonku

and i dressed right
for the smoke
will it wrinkle
if i fall?

Section Five

we are the fire that burns the country.
—bantu

odoni ki ipero
(no one plans alone)

Song No. 2

(1)   i say. all you young girls waiting to live
       i say. all you young girls taking yo pill
       i say. all you sisters tired of standing still
       i say. all you sisters thinkin you won't, but you will.

       don't let them kill you with their stare
       don't let them closet you with no air
       don't let them feed you sex piece-meal
       don't let them offer you any old deal.

       i say. step back sisters. we're rising from the dead
       i say. step back johnnies. we're dancing on our heads
       i say. step back man. no mo hangin by a thread
       i say. step back world. can't let it all go unsaid.

(2)   i say. all you young girls molested at ten
       i say. all you young girls giving it up again & again
       i say. all you sisters hanging out in every den
       i say. all you sisters needing your own oxygen.

       don't let them trap you with their coke
       don't let them treat you like one fat joke
       don't let them bleed you till you broke
       don't let them blind you in masculine smoke.

       i say. step back sisters. we're rising from the dead
       i say. step back johnnies. we're dancing on our heads
       i say. step back man. no mo hanging by a thread.
       i say. step back world. can't let it go unsaid

haiku
  (for mungu and morani
  and the children of soweto)

may yo seasons be
long with endless green streets and
permanent summer legs.

An Anthem
  (for the ANC and Brandywine Peace
  Community)

Our vision is our voice
we cut through the country
where madmen goosestep in tune to Guernica.

we are people made of fire
we walk with ceremonial breaths
we have condemned talking mouths.

we run without legs
we see without eyes
loud laughter breaks over our heads.

give me courage so I can spread
it over my face and mouth.

we are secret rivers
with shaking hips and crests
come awake in our thunder
so that our eyes can see behind trees.

for the world is split wide open
and you hide your hands behind your backs
for the world is broken into little pieces
and you beg with tin cups for life.

are we not more than hunger and music?
are we not more than harlequins and horns?
are we not more than color and drums?
are we not more than anger and dance?

give me courage so I can spread it
over my face and mouth.

we are the shakers
walking from top to bottom in a day
we are like Shango
involving ourselves in acts

that bring life to the middle
of our stomachs

we are coming towards you madmen
shredding your death talk
standing in front with mornings around our waist
we have inherited our prayers from
the rain
our eyes from the children of Soweto.

redrain pours over the land
and our fire mixes with the water.

give me courage so I can spread
it over my face and mouth.

haiku
(for johnbrown)

man of stainedglass legs
harvesting the blood of Nat
in a hangman's noose.

A Poem for my most Intelligent
10:30 AM Class / Fall . 1985

it was autumn. the day insistent
as rust. the city standing
at the edge of confessionals.
i had come to this room from other
rooms. footsteps walking from
under my feet. and i saw
your faces eavesdropping on shadows
rinsing the assassins from your eyes.
and our legs genuflected
beyond pain. incest. rage. and
we turned corners where the scare
crow smiles of priapus would never
dominate. and we braided our
tongues with sequins gathered
up our mothers' veins in
skirts of incense. what we
know now is that the coming spring
will not satisfy this thirst.

haiku
    (for paulrobeson)

your voice unwrapping
itself from the congo
contagious as shrines.

Introduction

1. Ngugi wa Thiong'o at Temple University

At night the noises of Kenya rise: cries of children and workers. Politicians and workers. Patriots and workers. The incessant lights of american military bases bleating like lost stars in the night. And the country. Loud with corruption. Continues to hide behind international conferences for women. And in the prisons and villages and cities, poets and professors dream of freedom. And their dreams and hopes, silhouetted against a country with skeletons coming out of its head, whisper. We are coming. Eating a little earth. We are coming to stop the imperialists incessant dawns.

Ngugi has eaten a little of this earth. And yes. We all have to eat a little earth before we die. And we who come from the earth will finally taste of ourselves. This earth. Which will seep from the corners of our mouths and make us whole.

Introduction

2. Ngugi wa Thiong'o at African/Am/Studies

As I read Ngugi now it seems as if his words have taken on more flesh and are more human. They have become larger. His men. Women. Moving. Stumbling. Resisting. Plunging into everything that is delicate.

And through his words. Through this kenyan man. Black and still with sun. Eyes in spreading solitude. And thru this Kenyan man. In exile from his country. We situate him in closer contact with the Philippines. Nicaragua. Cuba. The World.

Like Jose Martí, he is a writer and patriot. He writes of his landscape and believes as Bruno Walter and others, that good is "apparently destroyed by others but they do not destroy it completely, as evil destroys itself."

As I read Ngugi wa Thiong'o my eyes put on more flesh and i taste the world. There is no turning back.

For Mildred Scott Olmstead

When Andrew Zondo approached the gallows of Central Prison in Pretoria his last words were, "Know that life is not an end in itself."

We are gathered here tonight to honor a woman who has known that life is not an end in itself. But rather that life is a beginning. A constant coming and going. Where the eyes take on different accents and become more human.

We are here to pay tribute to Mildred Scott Olmsted: our permanent guest of this century. A woman whose body has sung several notes: the agitation of Jane Addams armed for battle against war; the words of Woodrow Wilson grafted towards the League of Nations.

She has seen imperialism spilling out from islands steaming across the earth like feudal lords.
And she has seen the impending death of imperialism.

She has seen countries plunged into misery, howling with people abused and abusing all that is sacred in life.

And she has called out against the altering of the rhythm of human life.

And she has taken no shortcuts.
She has laid out on this earth, piling up the years with risks.
She has thrown her head back with laughter and quilted each day with new sisters breathing green breaths from around the world.
She has broken the stereotype that the world has set up for women.

"When I am sick," said Yeats "I think of God. When I am well I go to the beach to play ball with the fairies."

When I am sick, I think of women like Mildred Olmstead and Winnie Mandela who by their work, ideas and dedication give birth to harmony. Who free us from the intoxicating thieves of this earth. When I am well I walk and talk with these women whose lives are wrapped in silk,
Whose words ordain us with prayer and peace.

Africa Poem No. 4

Another year. Children dying
wholesale in the streets
outlawed thoughts: arms
for youth. Guerilla warfare.
No crucifiction to confuse our young.
Land of adulteries.
Let us send guns to explode indulgencies.
No frontal checks.
Turning in my thirst
i see cities heavy
with abortions.
I tap it and tase
our flow. Sweet. Wasted
tapestry. Ah then an
end to sibilants. Blessed
are the warriors who
multiply. Together. We
will string our seeds
like viruses.

style no. 1

i come from a long line of rough mamas.

so here i was walking down market street. coming out of a city hall meeting. night wind at my back, dressed in my finest. black cashmere coat caressing the rim of my gray suede boots. hat sitting acey duecy. anointing the avenue with my black smell.

and this old dude. red as his car inching its way on the sidewalk. honked his horn. slid his body almost out of his skin. toward me. psst. psst. hey. let's you and me have some fun. psst. psst. c'mon babe. don't you want some of this?

and he pulled his penis out of his pants. held the temporal wonder of men in his hands.

i stopped. looked at him. a memory from deep in the eye. a memory of saturday afternoon moviehouses where knowledge comes with a tremulous cry. old white men. spiderlike. spinning their webs towards young girls legs and out budabbot and loucostello smiles melted. and we moved in the high noon walk of black girls. smelling the breath of an old undertow.

and i saw mama Dixon. dancing on his head. mama Dixon. big loud friend of the family. who stunned us with her curses and liquor. being herself. whose skin breathed hilarious breaths. and i greased my words on her tongue. and she gave them back to me like newly tasted wine.

motha fucka. you even offend the night i said. you look like an old mole coming out of its hole. take yo slimy sat ole ass home. fo you get what's coming to you. and yo generation. ask yo mama to skin you. that is if you have had one cuz anybody ugly as you couldna been born.

and i turned my eyes eastward. toward the garage. waking up the incipient night with my steps. ready for the short days. the wind singing in my veins.

Endings

for Black history month/February 1986

Spring. 1973. I was part of a cultural group from the United States visiting the People's Republic of China. It was Monday, we were singing songs on a bus, on our way to visit the Great Wall of China. One of the Chinese guides turned toward me and said, "Now, Professor Sanchez, we will sing one of the songs of your people—'Old Black Joe.' "

On that morning bus hurrying us toward steps jutting out from the land like enameled footprints, I took her hand in mine and stated: " 'Old Black Joe' was not a song by and for black people."

Even as I talked, though, I heard some white cultural workers disagreeing with me, with my sense of reality. My sense of history. Their words embraced "Old Black Joe" as authentic black culture and life.

My explanation prevailed, however, in that faraway place. My explanation about songs that depicted Blacks in ceremonial Sambohood. And on that morning resonating a global spring, I talked to the guide about spirituals and blues and work songs and blues and gospels and blues. And we smiled a smile of recognition, for her people had experienced in Shanghai park signs that read: "No Chinese or dogs allowed." On that Monday morning, we deported "Old Black Joe" from the shores of China to an uncharted shore.

My explanation prevailed because I explained how in unraveling the years of slavery and exploitation, I had to peel away misconceptions about Blacks, and at the same time gain strength from the life experiences and beauty within the culture.

And as I sang a blues song on that bus, I heard Lady Day's voice redeem our flesh contracting in pain.

And as I hummed a spiritual on that bus, I heard Paul Robeson's song get caught in my voice, drawing me up from deep rivers.

I explained how the myths had arisen. The myth of an American dream that promised to all believers a heaven of material luxury, personal liberty and an independence that could not be afforded in Europe—provided one had ingenuity, worked hard, was thrifty and of good moral character. The myth of the "lazy, vicious, contented, rapacious, violent black bufoon." The myth of black inferiority.

And I remembered Phyllis Wheatley's poem:

> Twas mercy brought me from my pagan land,
> taught my benighted soul to understand,
> that there's a God, that there's a saviour, too,
> once I redemption neither sought nor knew.
> . . . Remember Christians, Negroes black as
> Cain,
> may be refin'd and join th' angelic train.

I explained how a young country had reached out to images of "injuns" and "niggers," the cultural atheists by Western standards. The images were a warning of what one was not to become.

And I reflected on W.E.B. DuBois's manifesto: "Never before in the Modern Age has a great and civilized folk threatened to adopt so cowardly a creed in the treatment of its fellow citizens, born and bred on its soil. Stripped of verbose subterfuge and in its naked nastiness, the New American creed says: 'Fear to let black men even try to rise lest they become the equal of whites. . . .' "

Trees newly planted announced the Great Wall. And the hills stretched themselves out underneath the Wall like great sea shells under a great wave. The Wall, sitting empress style, smiled her ancient welcome. And I returned the smile.

On that Monday, as I started to climb that long winding trail of history and survival, my feet moved in tune to other feet. And I stepped inside Nat Turner's steps, and we heard together the patterollers riding, drawing nearer. And we ran. And I caught up with poet Robert Hayden's words and saw Harriet Tubman "way up ahead," her body cocked like her pistol toward freedom, her voice saying, "Hush now. I mean to be free . . . you keep on going now or die . . . Come ride a my train . . . mean mean mean to be free. . . .' "Wanted Harriet Tubman. Alias the General. Alias Moses. Stealer of slaves. In league with Garrison. Alcott. Emerson. Garrett.

Douglass. Thoreau. John Brown . . . Harriet Tubman, woman of the earth, whipscarred, a summoning, a shining . . . mean to be free . . ."

And the Wall, strutting her seams across the land, stood still as I arrived at the top. Stood still with the voices of the oppressed and the innocent. And I called out to Ida B. Wells-Barnett and Sojourner Truth, to Martin Delany and Malcolm X to Rosa Parks and David Walker. I called out to plantations and factories to the Birminghams and Selmas to police chiefs and dogs chasing black children at the moment of birth.

And I called out to Martin's dream to penetrate our bodies, to make us lean with legends and love. I called out to the dreamers to dedicate themselves to a new day, to discipline their lives so that the next generation could truly BE.

So I always smile when February comes, when Black History Month comes like thunder, blackening our skins. In spite of the cold, the agony of a gnawed earth, the horror of elected predators pressing our bodies against our will towards war and annihilation, I smile.

For I know as Martin knew: "The masses of people are rising up. And wherever they are assembled today, whether they are in Johannesburg, South Africa/ Nairobi, Kenya/ Accra, Ghana/ New York City/ Atlanta, Georgia/ Jackson, Mississippi/ or Memphis, Tennessee, the cry is always the same—'we want to be free.' "

For I know as the poet Margaret Walker knows that my people "are trying to fashion a better way from confusion, from hypocrisy and misunderstanding, trying to fashion a world that will hold all the people, all the faces, all the Adams and Eves and their countless generations. . . ."

And a new earth will rise. For we have endured and we are in spite of our wounds. In spite of our sorrow songs. We are. And shall be.

these are not good times for a black/woman/poet. these are times
where bright red public relations men market and sell death and
presidents in one day. All due respect to legionnaire's disease and
aids, racism is still the No. 1 killer in America. in the world. these
are days that leave you hanging inside yourself;

*i came up yesterday's stairs after him. screaming git outa here
nigger. outa my life. take yo books and clothes and git stepping.
And he turned and slapped me across mens smiles and brown
eyes that reflected softness beyond cotton smells. and i wrapped
myself in asylum wools and sweated out the years that never
happened;*

and the day was not just any day. but you shoulda seen it coming
in. Sun rays. dripping light like icicles on yo eyes;

*he was an artist that Malcolm/man was. he was a landscape
man he was, painting uncharted faces on separate plots. And the
sign said, no whites allowed. he was a portrait man he was,
painting me on a canvas called blackness and i slid on eyes with
him down his morning breakfast of revolution;*

the class was crowded. how to teach creative writing to 40
students? Amherst was a terrifying time for me, not the town itself.
there was beauty laid out so expensively against the sky that men
looked cheap in comparison. but the death songs tatooed on mens
tongues rising as gold dust in new england classrooms. and their
women. bodies out of control ready to explode and burst into any
hell;

*and the poem came. one morning. tommy's poem out of eighty
eyes. and i smiled rivers there in the dry mosaic town.*

> *i too have gathered the moss from*
> *solemn nights*
> *and replanted them in lips of*
> *morning shadows.*
> *i have been a dream storer*
> *churning—*

pumping restlessness
from eyes grown ancient in our sour smells
i laden in leaves
have resurrected myself. . . . *

gots to keep the young writers coming . . . strong men, getting
stronger . . . as Sterling Brown said so very long ago;

i've been two men's fool. a coupla black organization's fool. if
ima gonna be anyone else's fool let me by my own fool for awhile;

i was not your mother though you thought i was, "poet with no
tools to accomplish a way in the world." i said talk and i will
listen. i said bleed and i will catch your drippings in this morning
cup. i said cry and i will cry with you. teachers and mothers do
not cry, you said, only young poets:

> *it is an unsacred world this*
> *where poets do not sing as priests*
> *in righteous tones exhorting the creator*
> *of the sun*
> *it is absurd this—*
> *this uncharacteristic and unseasoned telling*
> *that i would call a life*
> *in which each morning*
> *the earth falls away from my door*
> *returning only as i come home*
> *threatening to smash me under the threshold. . . .* **

the class was small but she was not. her green eyes bulged against
the Pennsylvania room where we sat each tuesday afternoon and
read our writings. . . . ;

> *far simpler than imagined,*
> *a glimpse sideways, the billowing*
> *over of straw hats*

*   Thomas W. Jones/Amherst College
** J.D. Williams/Amherst College

the flicker of an ash
and there can be speaking.
The sun is overheard
glittering at our chatter
at fine weather and explorings;
the preludes to more
than the hours of an afternoon. . . . ***

keep on turning out poets girl. we need them. the world needs
them. cuz we hear America singing . . . singing. . . .

it took me about ten years to do it
but i finally got the niggers, liberals, gays,
radicals under control. it's good
times again. . . .
i got my act together &
i'm coming out in drag
and with force
watch out . . .
cuz i fo sure believe
murder is more meaningful
than suicide. . . .

and his song is fo real.

*** Mandy Uhry/Univ. of Pa. College

Graduation Notes:
  for Mungu, Morani, Monica and Andrew and
  Crefeld seniors:

So much of growing up is an unbearable waiting. A constant longing for another time. Another season.

I remember walking like you today down this path. In love with the day. Flesh awkward. I sang at the edge of adolescence and the scent of adulthood rushed me and I thought I would suffocate. But I didn't. I am here. So are you. Finally. Tired of tiny noises your eyes hum a large vibration.

I think all journeys are the same. My breath delighting in the single dawn. Yours. Walking at the edge. Unafraid. Anxious for the unseen dawns are mixing today like the underground rhythms seeping from your pores.

At this moment your skins living your eighteen years suspend all noises. Your days still half-opened, crackle like the fires to come. Outside. The earth. Wind. Night. Unfold for you. Listen to their sounds. They have sung me seasons that never abandoned me. A dance of summer rain. A ceremony of thunder waking up the earth to human monuments.

Facing each other I smile at your faces. Know you as young heroes soon to be decorated with years. Hope no wars dwarf you. Know your dreams wild and sweet will sail from your waists to surround the non-lovers. Dreamers. And you will rise up like newborn armies refashioning lives. Louder than the sea you come from.